Dot to Dot Animals
Stress Relieving Puzzles

By Dottie's Crazy Dot-to-Dots

WELCOME!

Dot to dot books for adults are relaxing and fun. The directions are simple: Find dot #1, and draw a line from that dot to dot #2, and continue on. As you connect the dots, the picture will take shape.

Take your time and don't stress, there is always another dot, and you will always find it.

This book contains 20 beautiful animal images for you and 4 bonus images from another dot to dot book. We've also included a link to a pdf online where you can download and print the images from this book, in case you wish to connect the dots again! You'll find that in the last pages of this book.

We hope you enjoy this dot to dot book. We are a small, independent publisher and your purchase means a lot to us!

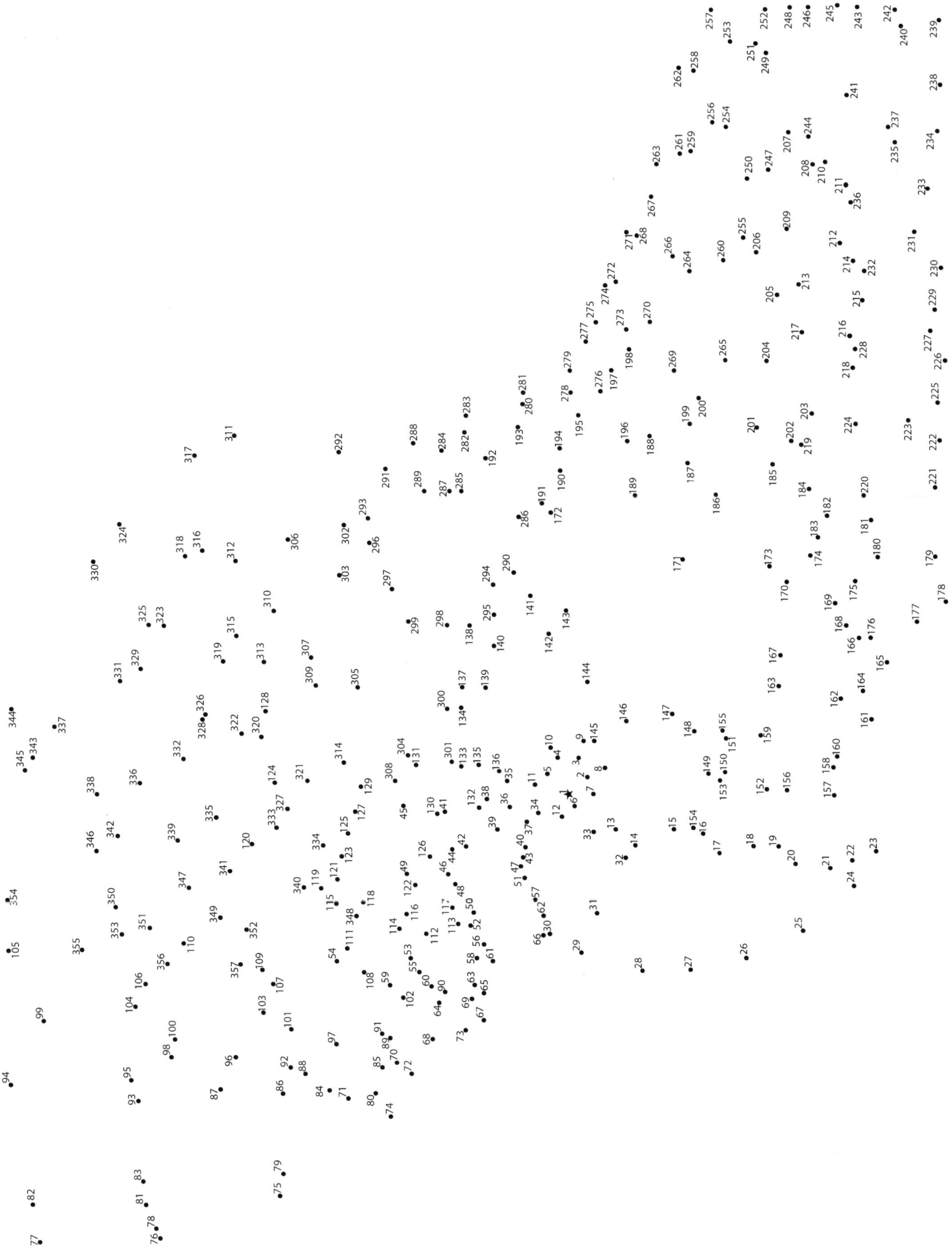

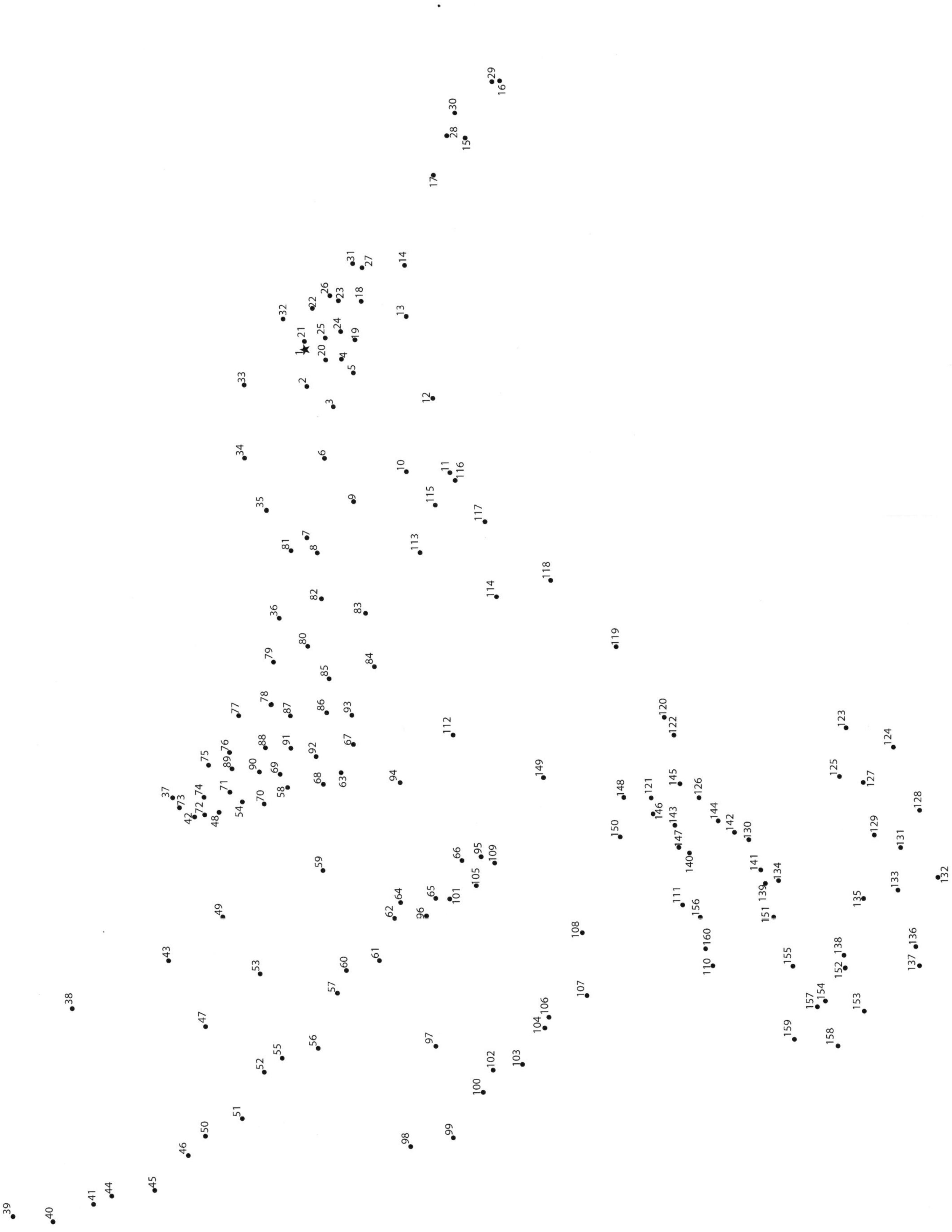

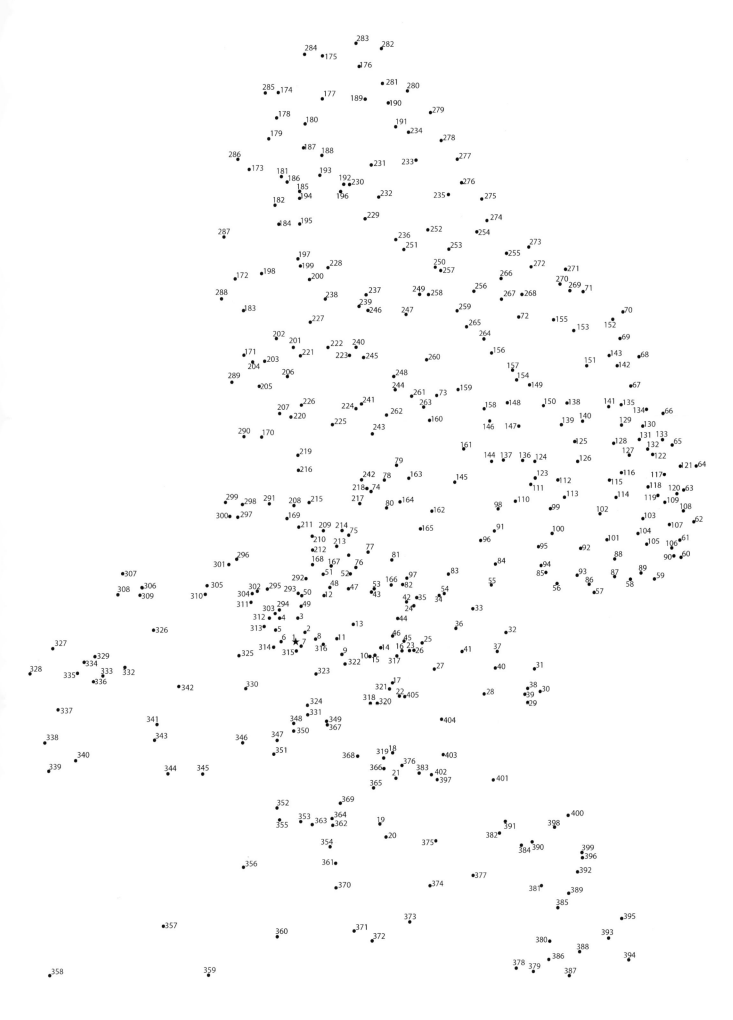

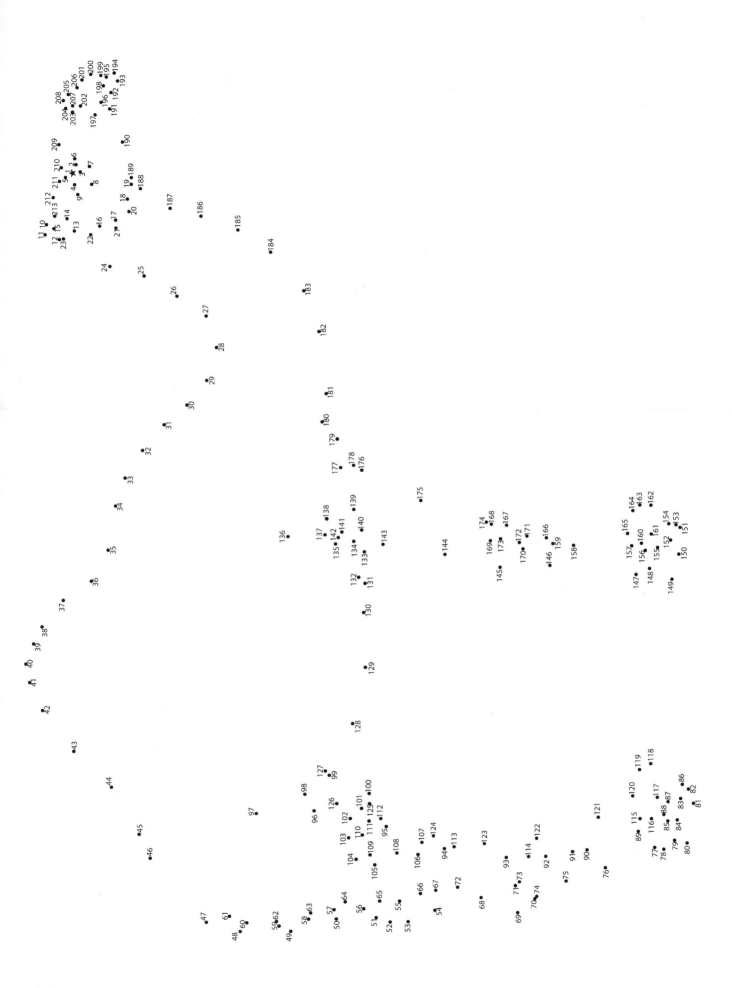

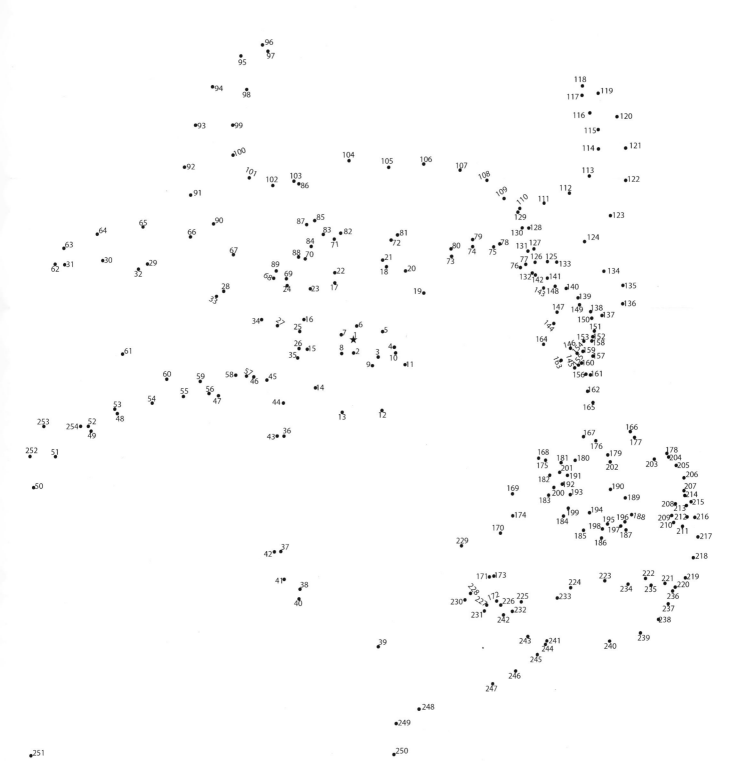

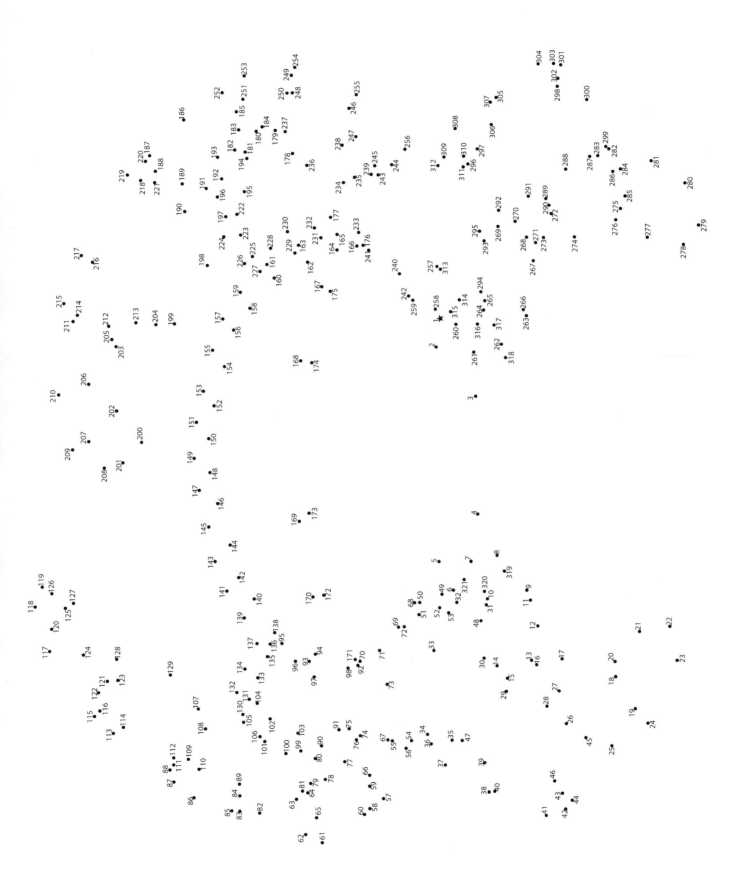

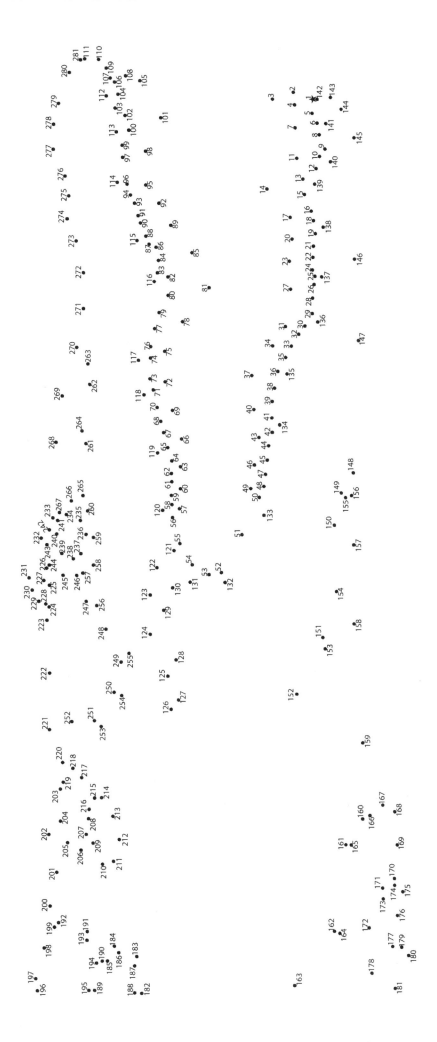

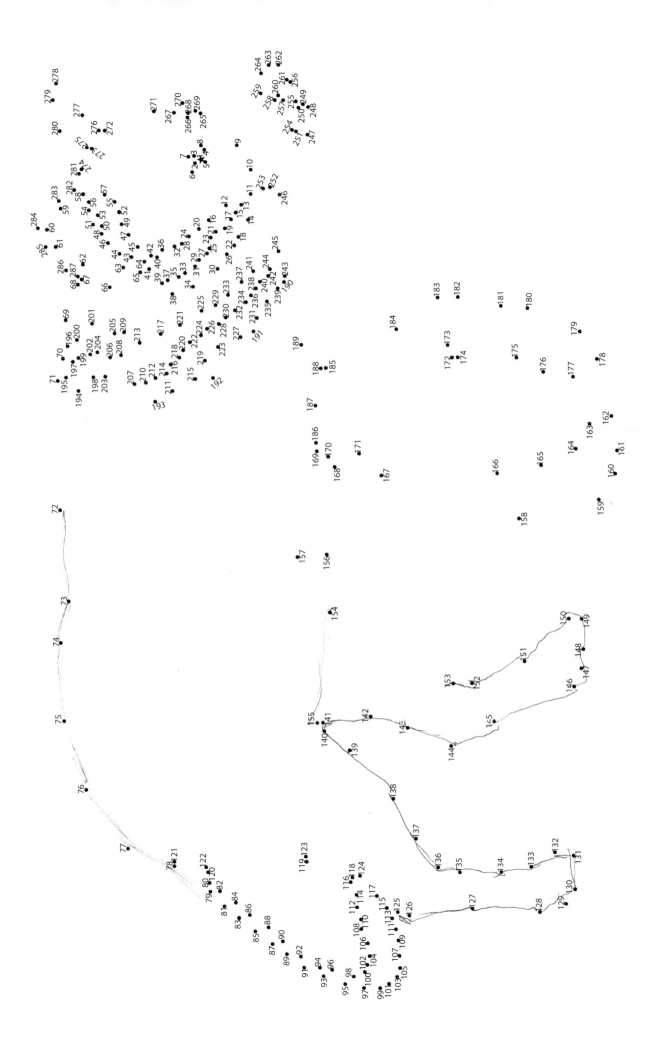

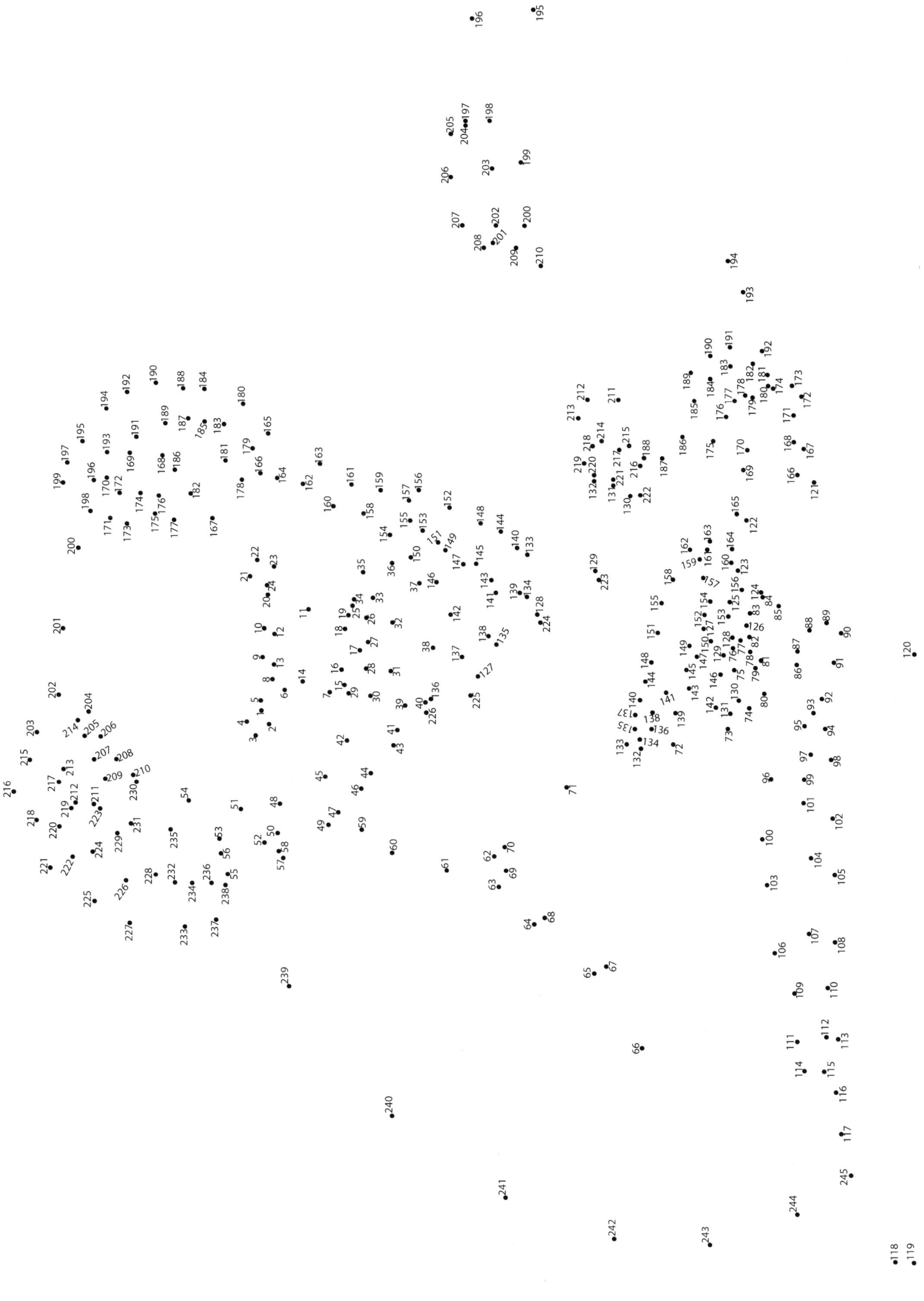

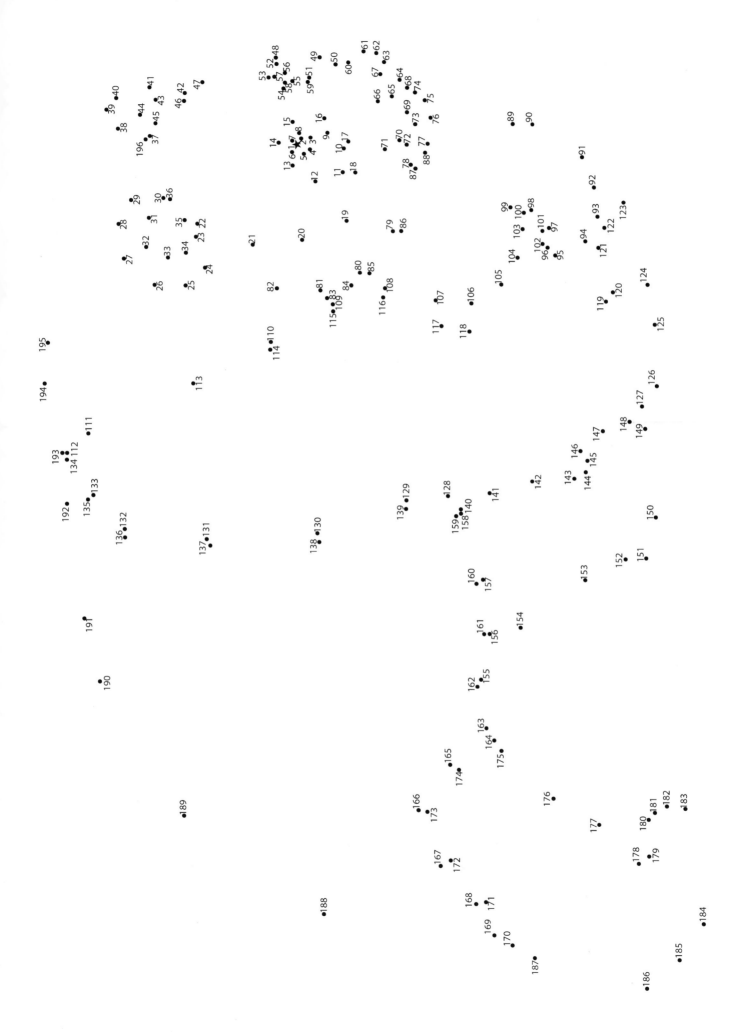

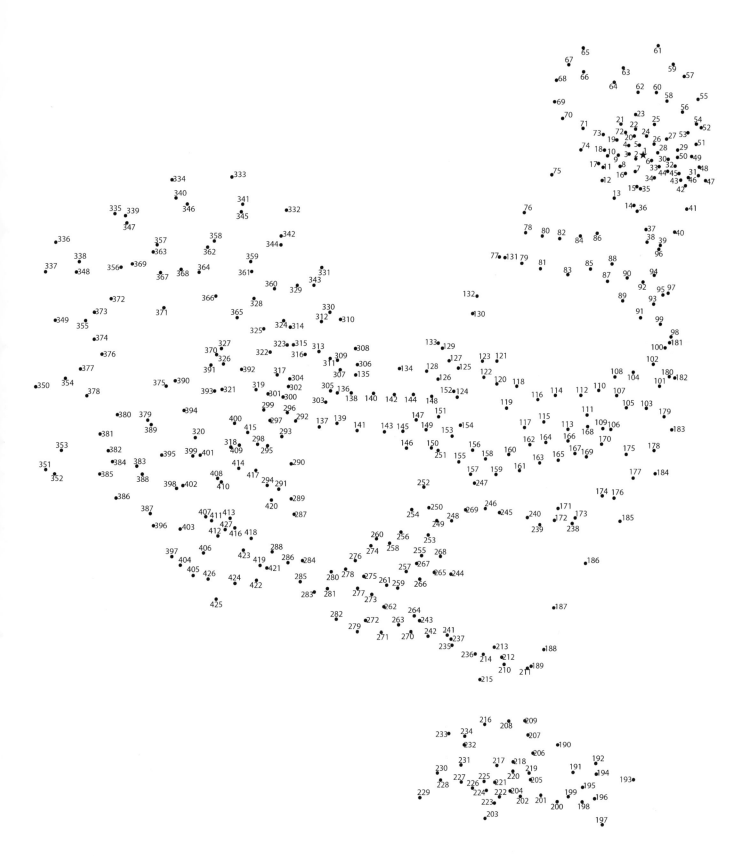

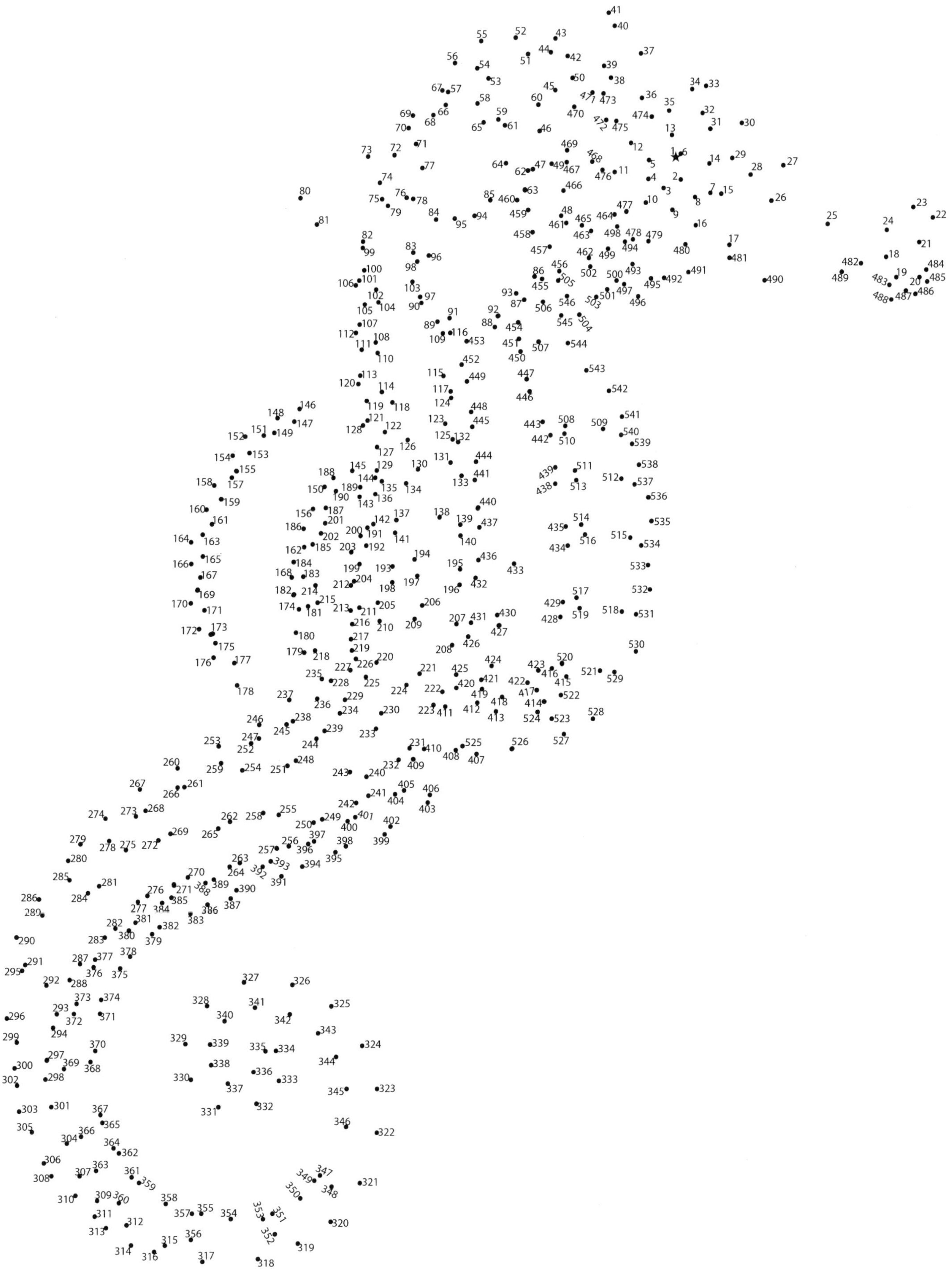

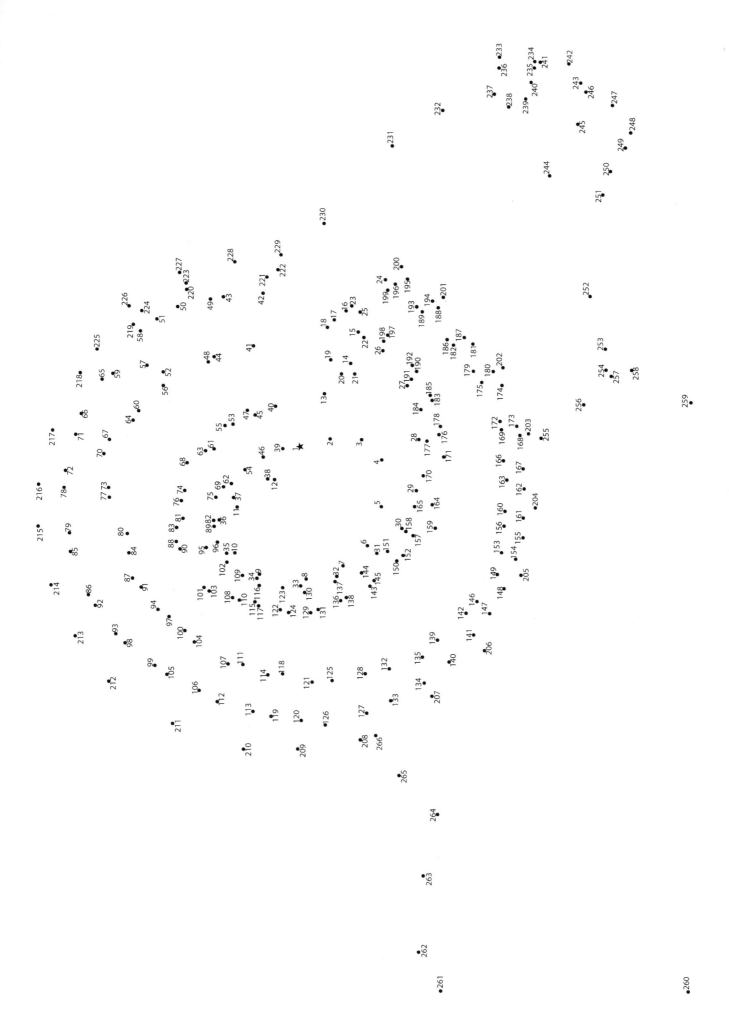

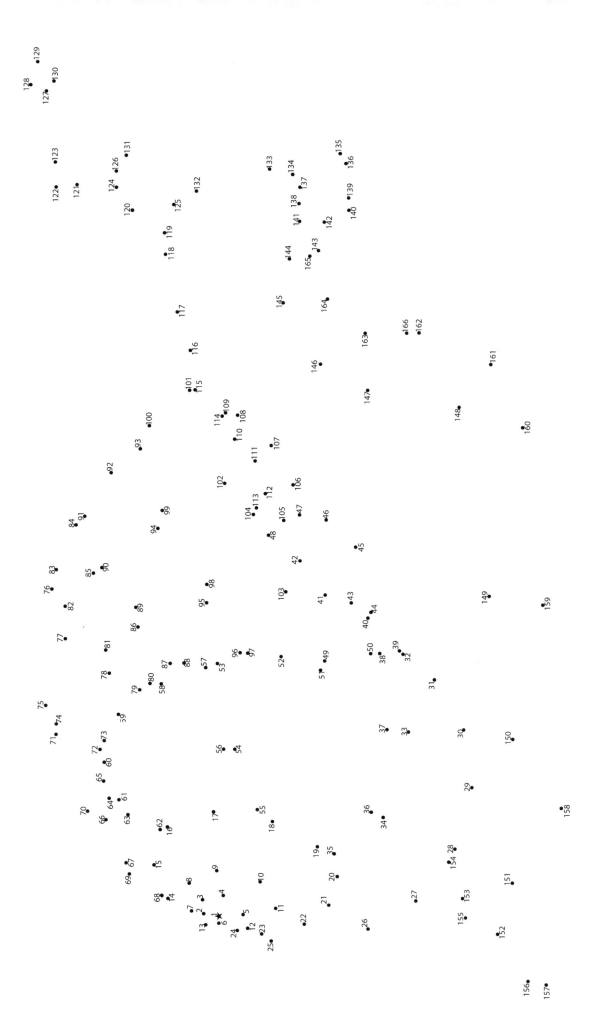

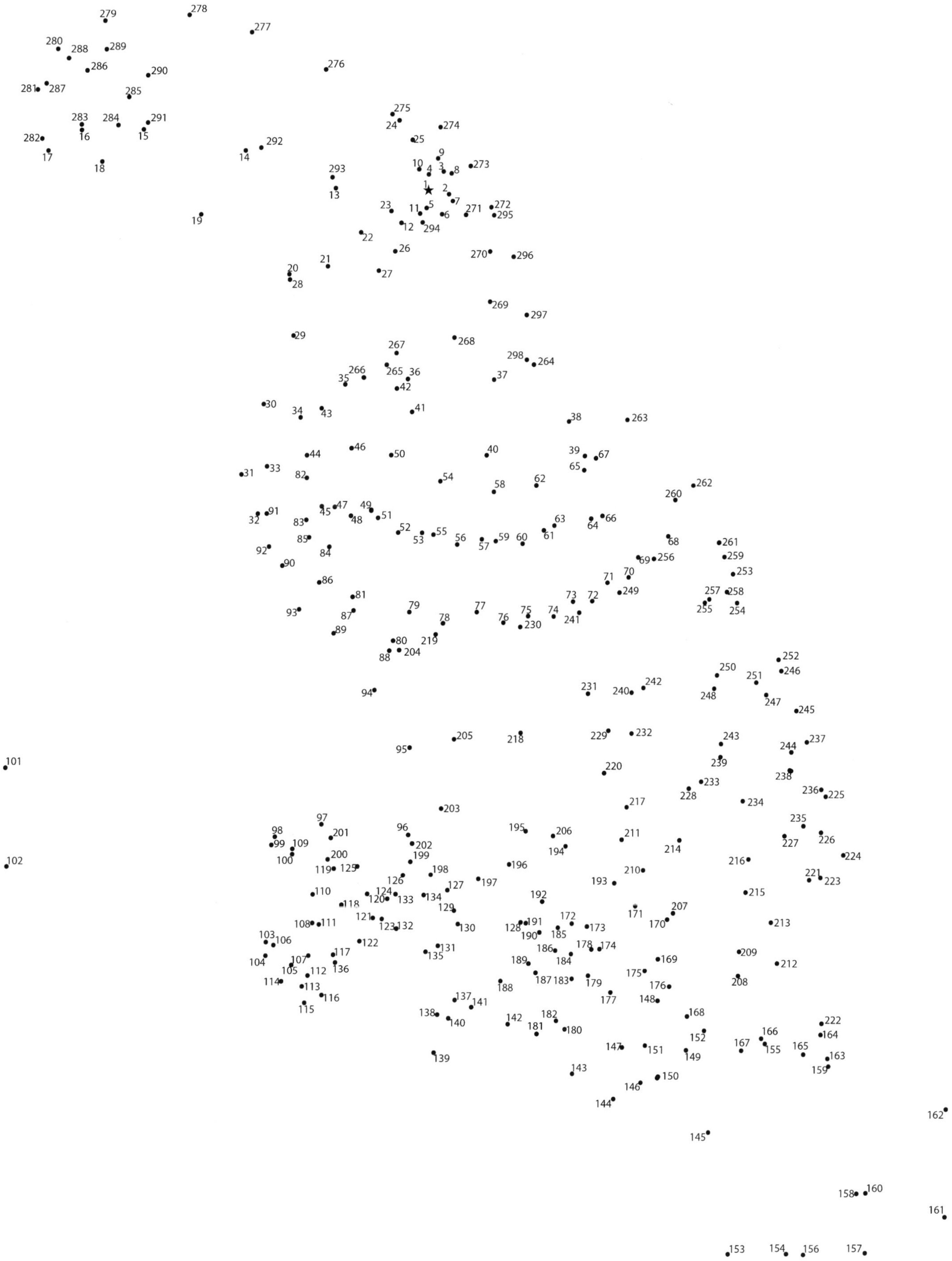

Enjoy four bonus images from Extreme Dot to Dot Animals on the next few pages."

Find our books on Amazon.

Extreme Dot to Dot Animals
Relaxing Puzzles for Adults

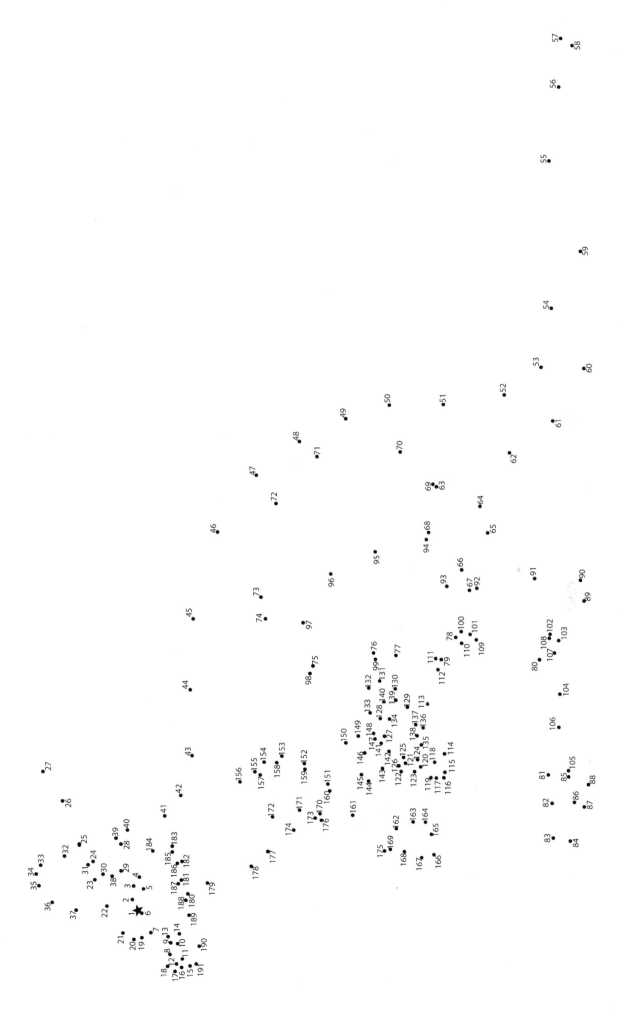

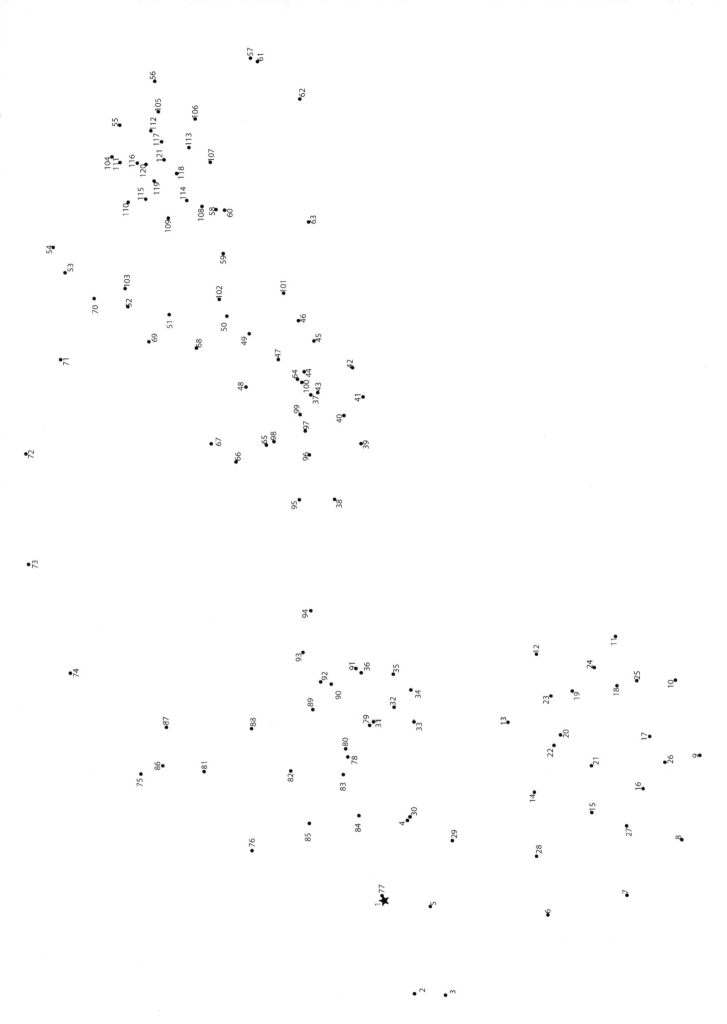

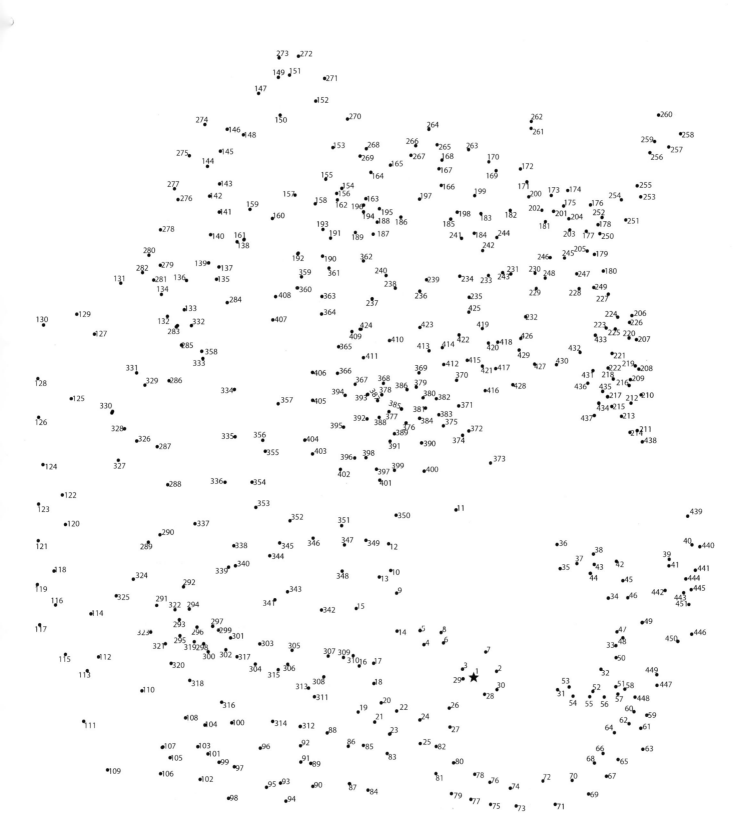

SCAN ME

Did you know?
We Have a Great Mailing List!

Free Downloadable Dot to Dot Pages
Monthly Giveaways
Exclusive Discounts
& More!

Scan the QR Code with your phone's camera
or visit DotToDotClub.com to Join

thank you

for your purchase!
If you enjoyed this book,
please leave a review. As a
very small independent
book publisher, every
review helps us compete
with larger companies.

Scan the QR Code
to Leave a Review

(open your phone's camera
and hold it up to the
square)

Made in the USA
Las Vegas, NV
07 August 2023

75782818R00031